Beau

Cancer Courage

When at age 42,
40 tumors were discovered, , ,

poems

Ken Buhr

Gabe's Dad

Garden Oak Press
Rainbow, California

Garden Oak Press
1953 Huffstatler St., Suite A
Rainbow, CA 92028
760 728-2088
gardenoakpress.com
gardenoakpress@gmail.com

First published by Garden Oak Press on September 15, 2023

ISBN-13: 979-8-9879532-2-8

Library of Congress Control Number: 2023938708

Printed in the United States of America

GABRIEL JOHN BUHR

February 28, 1975 — August 3, 2020

These poems were written during the year when my son Gabe became gravely ill with cancer and died. Beginning in April 2020, I began a streak of a poem-a-day that lasted 365 days. These 110 poems were written during that year. They are presented here with a father's admiration of that son and a father's grief for that loss.

These words have been good for me. Together we survive the assault on our lives from cancer, illness, and death. We become able to say *Thank you* from wounded, healing hearts. I give these poems to you in my son's name.

— KEN BUHR

CONTENTS

Beautiful Son

Cancer Courage

When at age 42,
40 tumors were discovered . . .

poems

Ken Buhr

Gabe's Dad

GARDEN OAK PRESS

Daredevils on a Tightrope

PET scan . . .
No longer impersonal words—
we live the imbalance of anxiety—
sadness—hopelessness.

MRI . . .
We move from word to word
reading, reflecting, discussing
with intense narrow attention.
We are daredevils on a tightrope.

Infusions . . .
Every move becomes threatening
while emotions veer inside us
focused only for . . . surgery
. . . radiation . . . chemo impact.

·

This train we're on moves fast—
    passing signs cannot be read.
We suffer flashes of who are we?
    where are we? who is with us?
    how far might we have to go?

We step away from the train
    befuddled—
familiar streets and offices
    appear unknown,
shops, the deli, and dining table
    perversely betrayed.

Borrowed from the Sky

Our smiles conveyed the sun
and the soft light of candles.
From decades of smiles
an inward glow, an outward beam
a brilliance illuminates each season.

Those smiles, a fortune's worth,
are ours . . . then and always.

I have wished for you,
have wished for myself
peaceful deaths
as though our final smiles
were shared emanations
from Chartres Cathedral,
the splendid blues and reds,
the sky alive in stained glass.

We Too Are Sculptors

Michelangelo's David,
    Rodin's The Thinker.
Stone speaks. Bronze
    instructs us.

Words and actions
    cast spells—

—a desire to speak
—a choice to linger
      in compassion
—a touch in sorrow . . .

we sculpt one another.

Newly Aware

This table where I sit
made of sturdy wood
seats four comfortably.

This chair, simple and firm,
helps keep posture healthy
provided I am mindful.

What about your chair,
your table, and these words?
They unite us now

following inner threads
in our lives of intriguing
length and meaning.

> An impulse like a whisper
> reconnects me to my mother
> who died age fifty-five.

> I respond to her presence,
> now in what I feel
> and think and see.

An awareness emerges:
  I live now what she
    did not get to live.

From this quiet reflection
a newfound energy comes.

The Beach Hat You Bought

Discarded medicines

the chaos of disease

the words we didn't say

thoughtless hurtful words
we never should have said

    so much weighs heavy.

This morning the beach hat
    you bought for me
narrowed my thoughts

the way a magnifying glass
    focuses light
sun-intensifying and fiery

the searing not lessened
by tearful sun-blind eyes.

Metastasized

Another scan— multiple sites—
results: "somewhat positive"

    any hope for a cure?
    Incalculable

merely a dismaying glimmer
in the maze where we wander

    questions unrelenting
    answers elusive.

The silent walls glare.
We sit. We crumble.

      •

Metastasis . . . Chemotherapy . . .
Positron Emission Tomography.

    Abstract terms have live feelings —
    dread, doubt . . . sad, weak, tired.

Radiation Oncologist . . . Neuropathy . . .
Edema . . . Experimental Trial.

    Together we breathe and live
    love love peace love love.

Best Life Ever

The four-year-old's arms-wide hug
    came in the good-night hour
with three perfect words clearly said:
    "Best life ever!"

despite earlier a tumble from her bike
    onto rough asphalt
a new scrape next to a healed one.
    Shouldn't pedal in flip-flops!

Fortunately the helmet did its job.
    Not today's only frustration.
But how fast she could go!
    able to pump even uphill.

Grandparents attempt to cope
    with their son's, her uncle's cancer—
endeavoring to appreciate beauty,
    embrace goodness

    supports, as we must be, to each other.

Granddaughter's words at day's end
    help to sleep and rest—
    "Best life ever!"

A Mere Sound

A patio door's click
recalls pleasant hours
and unperturbed days.

Sudden sorrow lurks
in the tap and swish
of approaching feet.

In the chaos of surviving,
I realize, I breathe!
as able to mourn loss

as to delight envisioning
a clear sky and seagulls
calling to one another.

Note: There is need for a new punctuation mark. After delight and after sky there is a slight breath, a pause shorter than the comma. It could appear as the upper dot from the colon and semicolon. Perhaps it could be called the *semicomma*.

Two Photos

Two photos lie before me
in each the intense beauty
of an earth-exalting sunset.
Spectacular colors ripple
in darkening river water.
How beauty congregates
for mankind and for fish
in life-engendering water
beneath the fiery crown
of an almost-evening sky.

One photo—a silhouette,
back view of a fly-fisherman
probing with cleverness and skill
the river's mystery,
abolishing dark and drab
strife and sorrow.

Second photo—the similar
sunset's blazing beauty
without the fisherman
his taut and active body
his carefully planned, chosen
far-flung alluring fly or nymph
his bending rod.

The void grabs me,
annihilates tangible
space and time.
Two photos . . . slay me.

Through a Train Window

In the moonlit darkness
there appeared in my window
a rather misty, gently jittering
reflection of my weary face
as though the face of someone
only slightly known to me.
This sight sparked interest
in this person's journey,
destinations near and distant
through switchyards pre-set
yet fraught with uncertainties—
this swift blurred ride
on unforgiving rails in the dark.

Soft Presence

Spare me these awakening thoughts
    our son in the middle of his gifts
    his passions, his goodness
how soon now his death?
Weeks? Months?

A paralytic onslaught
threatens another day.

My lungs' soft presence
    and the family cat
    snuggling and purring
persist

invisible strength
directing
    the camera of the eye
sustaining
    the life-shaping mind.

In our universal tread
    toward the grave
awkwardly moving
through the morning
    the afternoon
    the evening . . .
these steps
    persistently sufficient.

Hope Extends a Hand

Hope comes not
from pyramids, temples
    and coliseums,
from estates, spacious malls,
    and industrial complexes.

Humbly hope relieves
    doubt and weariness,
        stands bold in readiness
      to extend a hand
        a shoulder to lean on
          a heart to trust.

Visit to the Fishing Fleet's Pier

Saturday morning fish market with Gabe

Fresh ocean air recalls
first steps on a beach,
rhythmic crash of waves,
rush of awesome surf,
and dangling toddler body
    safe in parental arms.

A harpoon, a fishing net,
a line and hook, a lure,
evoke the catch's thrill
    muscles carefully tuned
    the mind's energy calm
a sense of timeless time
the flow of artists and athletes
moments of ecstasy.

We open piers of memory,
the ocean and ourselves,
harmonic lifetimes evolving
ebbing and flowing together
where circling seagulls glide and
endless waves pass gallantly by.

Dying Separately

I will not die with you,
though a thousand times
this wish taunts me—
yet to so devalue life
would stain love's courage.

I cannot die for you.
My fate is to live
much too soon without you,
then to learn how far
absence casts its pall.

If I die before you
you may read these thoughts
find solace in your loss
from these words inscribed
in love undying.

Intractable Pen

Waiting for spread-of-cancer results
during prolonged fourth-stage treatment

is like an unreliable ballpoint pen
scratching futile lines and circles
until the paper begins to shred.

    Desperate curlicues and slashes
    make the pages cringe and cry.

Nothing helps. Casting aside
    the useless ballpoint, crumpling
    the tattered paper—nothing.

Indeterminate waiting—drags on.

Play Hello with Me

Today I will desire

    everything of earth
       and sky
  river and shore,
     couch and table,
  becoming mine
  and shared with you

  desire's opposite—
     incurious mind
    passive stance
  buried deep
    as nuclear waste.

In harsh reality
    we still welcome
a frosty beer,
    a warm cup of tea
as long as we keep
    company.

Until desire is silenced,
  play hello with me.

Instant Dark

A slight touch topples
 a child's tower of blocks.
A slight bump causes the elderly
 to wobble and need support.

Slight the ripple in the brain
 that makes me slip
from composure and hope
 to dread and desperation.

Instant dark of night,
 antarctic cold
descends in our family.
 A candle-snuffer is coming.

A Crush of Wrinkles

It's hard to know how much deeper
    how much more crookedly
cancer will distort my son's face
    narrowed and thinner-skinned.
His smile speaks a crush of wrinkles
    and absurd physical weakness.

Two days ago a grandson celebrated
    eighteen months of life.
This morning he makes a game
    of little-yellow-ball-under-the-couch
for granddad to retrieve, while granddaughter
    creates with stickers a family beach scene.

I would wish this day to be pleasant
    a boat ride, fresh-air and fishing luck.
But the broad sea's storms are strong,
    unpredictable, irreversible, and long.

I build and rebuild my castles of sand.
    I pray to reverse the tidal invasion.
Waves encroach, cold and more numerous.
    The wrinkles engulfing him buffet me.

Lonesome Tent

Yesterday I was a damaged toy
today broken pieces of chalk
or a diaper (from an economy pack
of diapers), soiled and discarded

careening from here to there
fatefully, no sense of purpose
every hour infiltrated with
oppressive hurt and loss.

A tyrannizing pain forces
me to depart from my north.
Daily it commences again,
stifles desire for tomorrow.

Cancer clears all else away,
then erects an empty circus tent
where, on a ring in the center
alone—unprepared—I quake.

Our Portion of Dying

When death stalks a child,
    a parent, a spouse, a sibling,
defiling the bonds that bring life,
    death looms unjust and criminal.
We ponder and converse
    as best we can.
Weep with bare courage
    in sad and absolute grief,
weep with the power of music,
    heart-rending, stunning.
Weep deep, but not too much.
    Weep strong, but not too harsh.

21

Today

In fresh air and a Bluebird-sky morning
    I'm not walking for a downer poem.
I'm exercising to promote a healthy longevity,
    though chance will play its games.

The hillside field, once nearly blue
    in spring's profusion of tiny flowers,
has transitioned to a ground cover
    of pale bleached green.

The dirt path through the field
    narrow and seldom used
has footprints in powdery spaces and
    bicycle tread hardened in dry mud.

Dry dust that comes to life
    must become again dry dust.
Fixated on this thought
    I keep walking.

No tears reach the ground. Steps
    still avoid the trail's ruts.
But my body chills. Death clenches
    his ominous fist

around one most admirable,
    most dear, most near
someone as near as flesh
    can be to flesh and spirit.

Led by You

You give generously each day
    despite progressive dying.
Your cancer is not yet to die
    and neither are you.

•

A prolific fall of pinecones
    distracts from an ailing pine.
We survive through admiration
    of your daily acts of courage.

Memory of Your Smile

Specific facts about you, about us, I recall
  though many are lost to me.

Nothing brings you present more
  than times when you gazed
      into my eyes

          and seeing what you saw
          you brought your smile

          illuminating deep in me
          yourself, myself

those interactions, those moments
  painful yet smiling.

Attending to Beauty

Your reality is fraught with mystery
    to me—
how you, my son, face death
    with strength I find beautiful!
Yet with what oscillation of fear
    and daring, who can say?

In you I admire beauty
    in its three components—
through your revealing actions
    singular identity arises
with a proportionate clarity of form
    that I note and can name
presenting completeness, an integral
    giftedness.

Ocean shores, mountain forests,
    rushing streams cannot proclaim
their own beauty. The human spirit
    attends and embraces beauty—
beauty present in your flesh
    as tenderly as the future's birth.

Hallelujah and Goodbye

Despite the pendulum's
    calm, steady arc

despite equilibrium
    balancing weight and motion

despite beauty's perduring
    quest for presence

fourth-stage metastasis spreads

disrespecting the good of life . . .
    the jump-around, sing-a-song,
    throw-out-your-hands and shout
        Yes! Hallelujah! of life.

Time, who pauses for beauty
    who stops in amazement
    and praises in gratitude
now forfeits its lavish presence
capitulates in an irreversible
       Good Bye to life.

Ultimate Worth

The splendor! Blue sky, bright clouds
    above a shimmering river,
evergreen branches with prolific cones
    above glacial boulders . . .
beauty free and beneficent

        our gratefulness is immense.
                Our control, slight.

Death in prime years
    raises havoc.

        From others' lives
                and from their words.
        we can derive guiding strength
                an anchor for the heart.

"When through one person
    a little more love and goodness
    a little more light and truth,
    have come into the world
then that person's life
    has had meaning." †

---

† Alfred Delp: *The Prison Meditations of Father Alfred Delp*.

These words by a Jesuit priest were written shortly before
his execution in a Nazi concentration camp.

No Entry

As you walk
your lone avenue

I move along
on other roads

wanting
to join you

there . . . where
I cannot walk.

No Hiatus

Words fail.
   Resolve dissipates.
    Have I begun
      a lonely walk
        to my execution?

I Look Broadly

I look broadly at my son's life
    and I see
there was a lot of me in him—
    some of it good.

His vibrant body and keen mind
    convey his world.
His pack of sorrow aside,
    he engages our hearts.

I admire most what he himself
    determined to sculpt.

The Joy of Tragic Opera

At an outdoor table across the square
　　in front of the Pantheon in Rome
　　for drinks and talk before bedtime
while caught in cancer's ceaseless challenge
　　of blessed hope and life
　　of scary acceptance and dying
I'd hope to remember the words we said
　　even if they merely veered close
　　to the relentless concerns on our minds.
Instead I remember the street we walked,
　　a lone violinist playing in shadows
　　exhilarating drama, operatic melodies.

I knew it was important that we talk
　　that we take vacation-time
　　by extending a chemo interval.
It was important—how many meanings
　　in that word: important—
　nighttime in that iconic place—
　　bright lights—porticos in shadow—
sounds and voices freed from the city's
　　daytime rumble—passing revelers—
the wholesome goodness of togetherness
　　in sorrow, anger, and fear—
　　in caring, humor, and admiration.

The words I've either lost or never said
　　blend with the violin's splendor
　　for beauty, for joy, for time together
while the Pantheon's majestic stones
　　protect the faithful pursuit of present life—
　　love in the midst of loss and dying.

Discordant Death

When I begin to have answers,
comfort is ripped away
by raw feelings,
by more questions.

During death's assault
    breath and hands turn
        to daily activities

to ordinary kindness,
    to present chores,
        to effort sustained—

through these
    discordant death
        is irrelevant.

Hope under Siege

Vague words, evasions
off-putting smiles
mere glitter

at times the best
a terrified heart
attempts.

Peace in Sorrow

When confronting the worst
    of cruelties
is it possible
    to rail at cruel nature
yet cling to resilient earth
    for comfort and support?

Into a darkening cave
we are impelled
alone in our experience.
    Dire thoughts and feelings
    alarm and disrupt.

Guiding paths by others
    from long before us
    from those with us now
    from those to follow
assist our stumbling steps.

We regain some footing,
learning the best we can
    to rely on fragile strength
    together with our bonds—
miracles for peace in sorrow.

Damn Puzzle

A jigsaw puzzle, only twenty pieces
simple, smooth-cut, easy to assemble—
yet great rage fills the house
when an 18-month-old wails
and heedlessly hurls the nasty pieces.

Watching for death is stripping
years from me, refuting
wit and heart and vision—
pieces of me far scattered.

      My son, don't leave!
          No! No!
   Promise me,
         you'll stay.

Deathwatch—

as though we could
control the hours and days!

Dying defies calming tools
    and wise sayings
constricts the breath
    nullifies reason
releases mustangs
    in the throat.

Rampaging beasts
    scatter our thoughts.
Thunderous hoofbeats
    pound on all sides.
Ferocity dominates
    a dust-filled sky.

We are trapped,
helplessly watching
this stampede
we are in.

Two Forty-Five p.m.

you died

you were resting
wordless
at peace
in our final visit

words of love for you,
and admiration

promises for your family
from mom and me
we watched
and you died

thank you . . .
    thank you, Gabe . . .
    thank you

sorry, son
this is
so brief

later
I'll have more
to tell you

GABRIEL JOHN BUHR
February 28, 1975 to August 3, 2020

Walking Together

When death was coming,
    the coming was slow.,
Your diminishing presence
    evoked immense absence.
Each failing function
    began to scream finality.

Grimaces of pain—
barely formed words—
then your lips, silenced—
your fingers struggling
    to guide a straw—
    such tiny sips!

Dying's steps completed,
no more anxieties
    about your suffering
no more agonies near
    your evanescing body

This numb mystery,
    this awkward void—
I begin to move about
    where you are absent

with remembrance
    assuaging and beautiful:
son, toddler, student,
    husband, friend, parent.

You, my son, you and I,
    we continue our walk.
We shall always walk together.

Mourning

I wondered as I read the sports
if you watched this game,
your favorite NBA team.

"I'll give you a call"
was my thought.

That sports headline and my reaction—
probably the only part
of today's newspaper I'll remember

the transition I am attempting to ponder,
even to write about—

this exceedingly rough translation
this difficult to transcribe

hourly refrain
in my heart.

The Third Day

A half-dozen!
starlings crowd the birdbath
      shake their feathers
      fling water crystals
      to the sky
      and take flight

displaying the iridescence
      of shining quick wings
delightful scintillation
      affirmative vitality.

In the murky water of the birdbath
      my son's face appears
      painful and devitalized.
Heartless thieves stole him
      away to far caverns

forced him to abandon me,
      left a remnant, broken feathers
            dull and useless

myself
      misshapen pieces,
            discarded and useless.

To Love Again?

Untimely death came
    for our child of 45 years,
infinite love
    infiltrated by mortality
love's basic formula
    of both joy and sorrow.

Others' kind and caring thoughts
    show compassion
yet expose again the pain
    the trauma of flesh and love.
Now grief to me is infinite,
    to love again absurd.

Tug of War

Can there be relief
in this tug of war
between my grief
and you my other loves?

Stretched full length
on this taut cord,
mysteriously un-breaking
I . . . am . . . the . . .
    anguished . . . rope.

A Million Smiles

There was no other face like thine;
no other tears flow quite like mine.

Thirty seven point two trillion cells
formed your human-body-mind.
Your cells! How many did it take
to shape the chambers of your heart?

How many cells in triumph
gave your eyes their depth?
your voice its incantations?
your cheeks a million smiles?

From molecular multitudes
we achieve a revered union
in our unique wholeness
from heart to heart.

When I choke in love's grief
vast teams of my cells
stymie words in my throat
deftly make these tears.

There was no other face like thine;
no other tears flow quite like mine.

Expedition Leader

One who learns when insects hatch
    and streams are right for spawning
conveys a sense for mankind's pulse
    and wholesome future paths.

One who sees a weed in bloom
    with wonder and with queries
leads us to revere redwood groves
    and respect irreplaceable mulch.

One who cherishes a hillside's smile
    and an insect's ode to morning
human-scapes our earth for living,
    mind-scapes us for giving.

That Kind of Day

A shroud of cloud
that deepened
through the night
begins this day.

I have no say.

The late-arriving sun
back-lights the leaves.
Outside my window
the glad world gleams.

I have no say.

Weeping? Rejoicing?
What in these hours
will enflame my veins?
Or solace my heart?

I have no say.

Strolling alone
in a redolent place—
reminiscing—
what remains of me?

Too soon to say.

Numbed by Grief

Foods without taste,
bland and undesirable—
actions without feelings,
words that convey little

abstract trivialities
remote and distancing
from reality's bite,
our son's death by cancer.

Admiration for his courage,
the daily goodness of his efforts
during three years of treatment,
will bring solace later.

Without haste we first
must own the cruel grief.

Steep Way

A heat-wave has begun.
    I take my walk anyway.
The steep part says,
    Cut it short today.
    Don't go on.

A simple thought prevails:
    What would Gabe do?
my son, who would
    not often be stifled
    by cancer's inevitability.

On these hills where we
    explored, played
    and you grew up
I struggle with
    your absence
here and relentlessly
    everywhere.

Up the steep way
    you accompany me.

A Little Deformity

One cell in your body
spread its slight deformity
soon to domineer our days
and lay desolate our future.
　　Can faith survive?

That force, so tiny yet fierce,
became a virulent mob
seized you from our world
of kindness, joy, and beauty.
　　Can I thrive again?

Photos of dinner parties,
holidays, and anniversaries
outings with friends,
will lack your smile.
　　Can love not cry?

Time-Blending

I've placed a recent photo
   on my work desk
eight by ten, glossy finish
   splendid colors

like millions do
   on desks, in hallways
on night stands, dressers
   and kitchen counters

images of special events,
   family gatherings,
nature scenes, classic cars
   cartoon sketches

some with specific narratives
   of place and person
like this mountain-river-and-sky
   photo by my dying son

our passions intersecting within time
   timelessly—
last—as in "final and no more"
   lasting—as in "always."

Contemplation about Time

Our speck of time
   in cosmic history
flashes like the milliseconds
   of subatomic particles.

But to us our passage
   becomes powerful and vast,
a river from tributaries
   feeding a huge delta

our portion of Life and Time
   inevitable
   ever-mysterious
   transcendent.

Though recently deceased,
   you, my son,
through our awesome
   pairing in time
are as alive to me
   as I am to myself.

Flesh of My Flesh

When your muscles dwindled
when your cheeks hollowed
    and re-shaped your face
when your last breath passed,
    these happened in me.

I turn and attempt
    to resume my journey
like a ship re-embarking
    after a disaster
returning to home port
    without you.

Through still painful days
    I re-enter the grandeur
    of living planet earth
your breath still my breath,
    your spirit in my blood.

We revisit soft breezes,
    sunset on sandstone cliffs
where the rhythm of surf
    leaves soft music.

Although sobs cause my breath
    to stutter and stall,
my eyes share our vision
    for the spectacular of being.

Nightmare Station

When family members at a hub station
    for trains to far destinations
    board differently destined trains
it's confounding and sad—
    a loved person taken away
    by steel wheels on rigid rails

hastened apart contrary
    to our previous plans.
        No matter how lovingly
        how meticulously
            through shared endeavors
                we've formed each other.

Gritty Doubt

Grains of doubt, like sand,
    arrive in groups
to thrive annoyingly
    in any slot of friction.
Have I grieved well enough
    for today? or too little?
Perhaps my sorrow is selfish.
    Is it wrong to feel joyful?

Doubts find the tiny cracks
    in sanity
lodge there, endure the grind
    of helpful advice
and the universal truths
    of cognitive-behavioral therapy.

In sunlight shimmering
    on a glistening lake,
in blue-green ripples
    following a cruising duck,
in lilting waves of conversation
    along an evening shore,
in the ocean's ever-restless peace
    without grinding on myself
        I need to let myself be.

No Choice

To mourn and be social
    requires pretense
    painful manners
    forced etiquette.

To mourn and be alone
    inside windows dark
    and barred doors
puts life on hold.

Real choice, it's been said
    requires three options—
    an idea useful for some.
But I know only
    social or alone
and these split me in half—
    each half paralyzed.

Undaunted Steps

Realistically he had no chance to live.
Three years he hiked and fished
worked and traveled and loved
kept fifty chemo appointments
    stride by stride
    with death at his side.

I ate delicious fish he cooked
treasured photos he chose to take—
sparkling rivers, cloud-speckled skies,
and sunsets' bold closure of the day.
    Stride by stride
    I walked with him

the best we mere humans could,
bearing cramping doubts and fears
often our hearts breaking
even joy and beauty a challenge
    steadying each other
    stride by stride.

A Legacy of Sky and Sunsets

Tell me more about this son
    whose light uplifted lives
his flare for sunset photos,
    for dawn, rivers, shores,
the contagion of his quests
    enlivening others' passions
his smile a brilliance
    attested to by many
whose rays reached far
    despite cancer's shadow
his choices conveying
    the sun's vital energy
in our galaxy's arms
    of human lives and starlight.

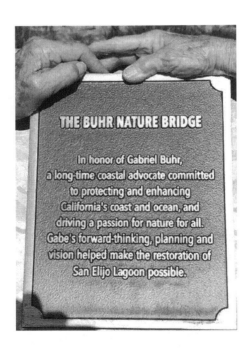

THE BUHR NATURE BRIDGE

In honor of Gabriel Buhr,
a long-time coastal advocate committed
to protecting and enhancing
California's coast and ocean, and
driving a passion for nature for all.
Gabe's forward-thinking, planning and
vision helped make the restoration of
San Elijo Lagoon possible.

Our Daily Rituals

We survive on "How are you?"
    "Fine. And how are you?"
"Don't forget, we need gas.
    Oh, and milk too."

Let us greet each other
    not as though
    we may never greet again.
Let us say goodbye
    not as though
    the last time.

The melodies in your voice
    join cracks in space,
    fill fissures in time.
Affectionate sight and touch
    tie up loose ends.

How do I know this? Trust me,
    you've loved me well.

Touch's Realm

In touch's realm we were born
    cleansed, nursed, and clothed—
moments that to us are sacred.
    When dying, we want touch.

Daily about many things
    we are attentive—
our array of emotions
    variable and energetic.

We share cascades
    of wished for inklings,
careers, talents,
    and aspiring hopes.

We pause from all these
    for births and death.
Life begins, life ends
    fragile—tenacious
    shy—lovable
deserving reverent attention
    and in need of touch.

We Carry On

We plod, we dance, we soar,
    across hours of bliss
of peril and sorrow
    of travel and leisure.

Each moment moves on
    like batons passed
sometimes smoothly—
    or quickly and at risk.

The race presses on,
    encounters hardships.
We gather ourselves,
    ascend together.

Death seeks control, roars—
    "No more time!"
Enduring many changes,
    we insist, "Let's climb!"

Wherever Gabe Went

You commanded the fish to bite
    and didn't doubt their compliance.
You studied well the bug hatches
    invited others to learn the skills
and share the thrills—fly fishing!
    hooked on fun and friendship.

When boulders gathered into cliffs
    and waters threatened your passage,
you threw the cancer in your pack
    shouted cliffs and waters down
kept on casting wisely chosen lures
    and brought us lovingly along.

Though a fly rod is still as useless
    in my hands as a violin bow
though beautiful mountain streams
    amid exulting pines are far
    from my sorrowful plodding
no place abides without your gifts—
    beauty's vivacity held close
    love's courage shouldered.

Trustworthy Moments

Time for the big game
   a storied rivalry
   much on the line
   rosters similarly deep!
Taking time for the game
   feels good.
Let's cheer our team to victory.

Within me contentment
   responds to the raw being
   of teams, venues, histories
the shared excitement . . .
   resilience despite losses.

If You Were to Read My Mind

Will I stumble through surges of pain
    yet sustain life's constant momentum,
still vital in me the music of laughing,
    loving, speaking, thanking?

        My pummeled brain
            cries out with questions
        pulls eyelids down,
            shuts senses' doors.

Insistent doubts demand
    black-or-white answers.
I wager much for ultimate closure,
    even staking sanity and health.

Our House / Gabe's House

When asked to set the table
    I get the placemats out
fold paper paper napkins in half
    light two tea candles

then suddenly I'm at

    Gabe's house
    to check the chickens

    water potted plants
    play with the dog

    bring food for Sam
    his once baby turtle

    the house where Gabe
    . . . no longer lives. . . .

Vision blurs.
    My heart sinks.
        I set the table.

My Chaos

Why do you leave me alone
in this pain? I need you.
Don't you care?

> I will handle this myself.
> Leave me alone!
> Give me space!

I'm a chaos of opposites!—
   leave me alone . . .
   don't leave me alone—
a struggling, self-centered,
   constricting, dominance
   of powerful feelings.

Endure with me.
This disruptive chaos
   that you see—
only for now is this me.

Hapless

The forest-green T-shirt with a Sierra Club logo
  feels okay—but not really warm enough.
The sweater, a blue tone more of night than day,
  feels okay—but holds too much warmth.

> Day leads into day since death took you,
>   and your absence seems to gnaw less.
> Distractions come with COVID-19 and wild fires.
>   Preoccupations create an almost peace.

The forest-green t-shirt that seemed so sure
  does not know what to do.
The hapless sweater finds no rightful place,
  tries to weep, but can't.

Parted—and Together

Gabe and I are conversing
as we do since Gabe had to leave.
I comment on how clear and fresh the air
    along the footpath near the lake
        where white birds nest on an island.
We smile, we reminisce—
    we talk, joke, imagine—
        and wish well for many things.

We are now in another layer of reality
    not found
    where eyes are accustomed to see
transcending the usual opposition
        of presence and absence
you, Gabe, vital and abiding—

your absence in the outer layer
    very painful
    as it will always have to be
your inner presence still awesome

entered when I push through grief's
    humungous door.
Each time to open that door
    I insert the key of what's been lost
    replay the code of regret and sorrow.

Then we saunter
    hesitant at first, but together
    in a large and rewarding estate.
Attentive to each other
    Gabe and I explore further.
After awhile we pause to rest
    take refreshment,
    and rise with zest.
Grounds and rooms are spacious
    and door leads on to door.

Going Shopping

I keep waiting for you my son
as though you should, you could
be with me, getting in the car
on our way to shop for shoes
and have lunch in the food court.

I don't know why I wait.
I can't fathom why at noon
the sun darkens, and how it is
moon and stars weep by day.
I don't move. This car won't start.

Death's Nemesis

You photographed and posted
    fifty chemo treatments
adding words of hope
    in whimsical metaphors—
ocean creatures gobbling
    cancer cells!

For almost three years
    you worked and fished
while death fussed
    and pestered.

Did you laugh
    at death? I think so—
also shouted and pleaded
    then laughed some more

    even made death
        put on ear plugs.

. . . Thank you, Gabe.

I Don't Know

Anger and disappointment
    pervade hours and days.
Sorrow and bitterness—
    will they prevail?
I strive to assert hope,
    sustain confidence.

Gratitude and awe
    integrate their part.
Peace, our drumbeat
    that I seek.

Visions of death intrude
    intrude
        intrude.

I mutter, "I don't know"—
    "don't know . . ."
        "don't know."

And the clock ticks . . .
    and ticks
        and ticks.

Desperate Prompt

My desperation spoke a prompt:
    "Practice dying today.
    This might ease the loss."

An early-morning walk . . . alone!
In the frying pan . . . only one egg!
    I died twice before breakfast!

Clearly there are many ways
to practice dying . . . none
lessens the heaviness.

In the miracle story we've lived
    and the places
        we've not yet gone,

        we will not
           be there
               together.

Caw! Caw!

Love for you continued
    painfully without you.

The kind presence
    of the living,
of family and friends,
    had begun a restoral,
and they had hopes—hesitantly—
    at signs of my recovery.

Caw! caw! caw! the crow's
    death proclamation
unsolicited intrusion
    no translation needed
calling again and again
    for you . . . for you.

The cawing of the crow
    be damned—be damned.

Prophet

"A drop of pond water can be full of life,"
    the biology lab-instructor advised.
My microscopic slide was quiet a good while
    until a symmetrical blob moved a bit
then suddenly was attacked by creatures
    too small, too swift to be seen
leaving a dented and motionless shape
    inert and disfigured—
    the miracle and fragility of life!
Six decades later I revisit that event
    still frightening, still enlightening.

In Montana, there's a river in partial shade,
    sunlight glittering on flowing ripples,
bright green pine trees on either hillside
    amid passing cloud shadows
all these in my son's photo, with peaceful
    purple mountains in the background.
This picture I decide to name "Prophecy"—
    my Oracle, my Sybil.

You took the photo on a family trip with friends
    only three weeks before you died
having dominated cancer for three years
    by your admirable spirit and vision
even as advancing metastasis in the last months
    dented and made frail your body.

You no longer go with me on morning hikes.
    But your courage radiates
clear and inspiring in this framed river photo
    beloved prophet in my life.

Deep Seams of Salt

Extracted from underground caverns
    or shallow evaporation ponds
salt is a universal capitalist
    the spicy lord at every table.

Salt trade routes, and exchange rates —
    I could pursue more knowledge,
if only such distraction could end
    my salt-filled flow of tears!

Daytime labor to drain ponds
    and mine long deep seams—
        nighttime for loneliness
            feeble wakeful hours—
                the slavery of salty tears
                    bountiful earth turned tyrant.

Widow's Hard Time

From your intimate and untimely loss
you endure a new level of trauma.
Others wonder how you will heal—

> Suzanne works to surmount grief
> in open solace-seeking ways.

> Eric bounces along with sudden slides
> into sorrow's quicksand.

> Emily deftly manages comfort
> through art she shares with others.

Your way is an enigma.
Do you already have a secret balm
    for your soul?

Am I needed as a confidant?
Or is it better, if I,
    reluctant and patient,
    stand aside?

We cannot imagine the keystone
that keeps your arch from collapsing.

Powerless

Cancer commenced
its slow progression,
soon enrolled militias
to roam and seize lands
powerless to withstand.

Everywhere we could
we fought, then fought
some more, as best we could,
accruing through months
daily tallies of desperation.

Overpowering
    that word
        again and
           again

overrides
    floral sympathy cards
    and kindly sentiments

infiltrates
    each well-meant
    caring, spoken word.

Heart Repair

Heart repair underway—
    not with a high-speed
      laser printer.

But hand-scribbles—
    crossed out, amended . . .
      no end to revisions.

Impetus

Unsuspected triggers
trip landmines of loss.
I've begun to anticipate
a relentless excruciating trail.

But for several weeks now
an appealing impetus develops.
At times I nearly rush
to revisit places resonant
with your vitality.

Yes, passage through the portal
of your absence brings pain,
now more quickly replaced
by the unexpected gift
  of your resurgent presence
    in a cloud bejeweled sky
      in a fly fishing photograph
        in the horizon sweep of my eyes
          in soothing moments of thought.
           Then even my breath is you.

Chalice of Loyalty

After death's severance
will I be loyal to you
when I don't hear
your footsteps?
When your voice fades
like blown dust?

While we shared
in the dailiness of work
household, family, and pets
we were often distracted

from talents and passions
from gains and resilience
from goodness ripening in us
    over 45 years.

You still give.
    You bring beauty
      grief's healing
          serendipitous gaiety
            intense spirit
   and I grow intensely
      in loyalty
         to the truth of you.

When the Light Is Right

There is a time in late afternoon,
if I pause, when I have observed
    sun rays between the vertical blinds
shining across this desk top
    onto an 8x10 framed photo
a wild river and shaded pines
    from my son's eye for beauty.

Call it an optical illusion—
or a miracle. Before my eyes
ripples flow, sparkle, and delight.
    The sun's slatted light gives
    the river water living motion!

Your final trip, from California to Montana
was exceptional. After nearly three years
    of chemotherapy, when it had begun to fail,
you were there, a group from three families,
    only weeks before your last breath.

True to yourself
    you sought beauty, dared to live.
My heart
that crushes on a rock in the river's current
    comes together on the other side

under scattered, fluffy, bright clouds
    that bring a special delight to blue,
the blue of the water, the blue of the sky.
    Together we create the beauty of life.

Challenge

Picture death as laughing.
What's the joke?
Is there something we don't get
and no one can tell us?

Death smirks at our dread
throws down a challenge

either block out death's mystery—
    yet live pursued and haunted
    by inevitable nothingness

or despite death's immanence
value our selves—who think
    and create the good of goodness,
    this day's kindness and hope.

Joy, yearning, striving, trust—
our living made more intent
by death's provocative leer.

From reflection we rise in awe
body swaying, dust rising
in the dance of beauty! vitality!
under both sun and moonlight

only seeming to dissipate.
A wind, as though a holy spirit,
visits and raises all up again
    as happens
    once more and always.

Together We Can

Death looms close at hand—
    covid-19, terrorist attacks,
cancers, global warming,
    starvation, massacres.

Dark voices predominate
    broadly and vociferously
yet light awakens at dawn
    shines on every human

the lowly and the powerful
    equally gifted to know love,
to admire courage, respect morals,
    share beauty, sustain hope

voices in communion—
    insights and worshipful awe
death harmonizing with life
    in summons and completion
the human spirit comprehending
    and sharing what each can.

Your Legacy

You have had to leave us
but a bridge bears your name
The Buhr Nature Bridge
part of California's coastal trails.

Here restored Pacific tides
flow to best rejuvenate and
nourish San Elijo Lagoon.
Birds nest, fish come and go
seagulls circle, heron's hunt
in this lush, peaceful lagoon.

We are not in Rome at the Arch
of Constantine or the Arch of Titus.
Nor in Paris at the Arch of Triumph.
We stroll The Buhr Nature Bridge.

We cross this gently sloping arch
over cleared waterways bringing
ocean freshness to tidal pools.
Children gaze and frolic. Hikers,
runners, and meanderers smile

and celebrate prodigious nature
cared for by your generous passion,
a span we visit with awe
and take our thankfulness home.

82

White Crane, Osprey, and Tide

San Elijo Lagoon, Cardiff, CA

Please, sit with me, here
where the tide flows in
and turning flows out

but now, unmoving
rests beneath the bridge.

We can be awhile here
still as the white crane
standing in the shallows
poised and pensive

or pausing like the osprey
on a pole high above
cleansing its feathers
with careful talons.

Whatever of bold and brave
we need, sit with me.
Rest first, like the tide.

Keeping Busy

I become busy when I have
nothing to do

dreading what might fill
the empty spaces

where once you stood
and held my gaze

or sat and held my heart
in both your hands.

First Thanksgiving without You

Others expect us to feel sad.
And we do.
Your life shortened,
    ours prolonged without you—
this screams unfair.

To dwell here, to desire, to love
and not yet to die
brings bitter sorrow and guilt
to our family table.

Assembling toy train tracks,
one missing segment
displaces fun and festivity.
One piece seems all.

Gathering Ourselves

From remnants
nurturant earth makes
imperfect beauty of it all,
provides us the art
to heal the wound
and bear the scar.

Failed Eulogy

What should I say?
    Thoughts about you
    overwhelm me.

Like in a hurricane
    familiar avenues
    become impassable.
Yards and streets—
    nothing the same!

Houses and cars smeared.
    Everywhere a dull grey.
Our flower beds
    under gory mud.

It's all too fierce,
    too sad.
I try again to rehearse
    words of remembrance.

I may have to murmur
    "Beloved to many"—
        if I can
            if I can
                if I can.

Don't Die, My Love,
Though I Know You Must

Love is a strong brew,
dares caring's heights
closer, closer to the pinnacle

until a chasm unsurpassable
blocks further passage

hope and despair
    together
desire and loss
     side by side

—I have embraced both
in knowing, loving you.

Blessed Burden

After your gentle parting
    I keep you with me
a mystery
    by which I live.
I hold you in my hands
    in mind and heart.

Looking back
    I am burdened by loss.
I turn my thoughts ahead,
    try to lose your presence.

To turn and move away
    but where to go?
Farther I would not move.
    All I want is here—
you with me—awesome.
    I command myself, Stay!

First Events without Him

Holidays. Birthdays

The backpack of loss on my shoulders
    is heavy, filled as it is
with good and beauty from his living.

I gladly bear its weight
    through slow and fast hours
    over uphill and down.

He was, he is the most
    admired feature of my earth,
as present to me
    as this pen and desktop.

            He holds my gaze
            to uplift this life
            until he die
            with me.

Resurrections

Feeling bereft of you
  I focus on my body,
let breath become
  long and soft

perhaps a yawn or stretch
  in quiet awareness
moments emptied of myself
  when you return.

Mortal sobs recur
  but you breathe in me
resurrecting
  the sun's warm gifts
   and our real bond.

I learn to trust
  love's undying.

Living Surf

Remembering our ocean-loving,
  surf-seeking,
    lobster-diving son

      creates a vision
        of waves and surf

         forming
          breaking
          faithfully

            both bright and dark
            this beauty.

Still Too Soon

To banish grief I scrubbed it
    off the kitchen counter.
I dungeoned joy
    behind a cupboard door.

Friends bring us chocolates,
    and spicy home-brewed tea.
Please . . . bring also . . .
    patience.

Your Photos Are Mine

Photos of you—infant son,
   graduate, husband, father
flash like shooting stars
   and campfire sparks
brief intruders in the dark
   of your absence.

Photos taken by you
   a far different story,
wonders noticed, cherished,
   preserved by you—
sunset glow on the faces
   of friends at the ocean,
a dawn photo when the river
   enfolds a fly fisherman.

                    I love you, my dear son.
                    These are our tears.
                    In joy and sorrow
                    we share.

Yes . . . photos by you!
   our gaze united!
We revel
   in nature's theater.
Our lives savor
   divine sweetness

until a lasting serenade
   and loving lullaby
shall close our eyes
   and bring us both to rest.

Closure

We are encouraged to seek closure
as though somehow we fail
when we continue to suffer.

Many suggestions are offered—
better ways to think, tools to use,
skills to practice. But these
and effort have not brought closure.

There still remain grief's impulses—
    anywhere—anytime
    nagging—commanding.

Carry on!
through what we know
of joy and sorrow,
of our selves and one another.
Hang on!

Only my death will be closure.

Days of Dust

Despite steep-scrambling feet
    and struggling mind
the darkest feelings grab faster,
    drag everything down.

Some people resume
    a wholesome pattern,
but my endeavors are out of step.
    Opportunities all prove futile.

I admire their accomplishments—
    then observe myself:
my mind, my body—I am
    an agony of dust . . .
        dust . . .
            dust . . .

Shadows and Radiance

The world goes on . . . without you,
    My world now—dismal—
thrashing without purpose,
    floundering in murk.

Or do I stand with you on a summit
    amid vistas clear and far?
Wherever you breathed and worked
    you brought vision.
You were responsible . . . and beautiful,
    not possible to understate how beautiful!

You ventured into each day . . . brought
    excitement, humor, and friendship.
You bequeathed worthy and loving gifts
    even when dying.

Floundering? . . . Or . . . summiting?
    Where will I find myself?
Can I find strength to choose?
    Often I don't know.

I promise you, I will listen
    to detect your summons
both from your own shadows
    and from full radiance.

The mountain is steep
    and defiant.
You . . . your spirit and I . . .
    we go on.
You state—definitively:
    the view is worth the climb.

Ghost-Making

Weighing evidence for ghosts' existence
sometimes convinces me, sometimes not—
and has left a sense of something real
yet different from the question posed.

Surely you have not become a spook
with malevolence contrary to our love.
Nor have you appeared as a helpful ghost
to guide me out from misery.

My son, my son, today grief
hits like a winter avalanche
dominating me and everything.

Solace and recovery will come,
I trust, from months making the shift
from acknowledging your absence
to sharing once more your courage.

I am sitting now at the dining table
with writing paper, assorted books,
cooled coffee, and flowers from our yard.
In coming days—sometime fairly soon

I will visit some favorite places—
a mountain trail, a fishing pier,
a bridge for strolling above a tidal flow
where sandpipers and white cranes wade.

In life's current of opulence and sorrow
I'm sure you will come to join me,
you, through your spirit, with me—
you, the kind presence of my making

> and I shall say again,
> Dearest love, I thank you.

A Man of Absences

I have become a man of absences.

Little matters to me
    the sunny crispness of spring
    flowers' midday exuberance
    the excitement of this moment!

It could just as well be autumn
    bold leaves in red and gold
    time for Octoberfest
    days and nights of singing.

Little matters—
    smiles perversely connect me
    with the loss of holidays and joy.

Others mean to help, tell me:
    "This stage of grief will pass,
    as it did for so-and-so . . ."
Don't engage my reason. I hear
    only prompts triggering torment
    unconscious and deep.

But please . . .
    stay somewhere near.
Your simple presence saves me
    when I am able to bear it.

Simply Aware

I'm tired. And I live
    with contradictions,
the nerves of my body wrenched
in extremes of joy and sorrow,
    of love and death.

I succumb to the convenience
    of irritability and blaming
watch increasingly
    for your inadequacies
even while I further doubt
    and blame myself.
(Distortions of reality,
    I am convinced,
    are yours, not mine.)

Such are my wild excursions
    in the grip of grief.
At times I'm able to perceive
    gentler, broader dimensions,
    acknowledge ironies
am more comfortable
    with your limits and mine.

Love and death's pairing—
    supreme gift . . .
    and imponderable cost!
I commit, as best I can,
    to the calm insights
    residing in deep love.

Measure of a Person

—how far
    thoughts'
      horizons
—how wide
    intention's
      extent

     •

—how loyal
    love's
      commitments
—how courageous
    compassion's
      sacrifices

Still with Us

Because he knew us
and we knew him,
    we know him now.

Because he loved us
and we loved him,
    we love him now.

Dread and Consolation

A former hearse
    repainted hospital white
      or loathsome grey
invokes a harsh presence
    of dying, death,
      and grief.

After heroic striving
    in either the briefest
      or the longest lives

after the mind's quest
    the heart's desires
      and the body's loneliness

solace comes
  with the communion.
    we find in each other

      and earth again supplies
        smooth seas, warm currents,
        and favorable winds.

White Cloud of My Son

White cloud of my son
amid sky's awesome blue
    watches over me

preceded by hosts of clouds
who walked the earth
    before us.

    •

We trek in his company
with one human people
    on this our earth.

This soil, these paths,
this room made sacred
    by all lives,
    by our lives.

    •

White cloud of my son
amid sky's awesome blue
    watching over me

my heart wants to burst
through this wall of ribs
    into music and dance.

Three a.m.

I awaken in the middle of the night
restlessly strive for needed rest
while walking on thin ice
with torrid feet
at 3:00 a.m.

Many Roads Together

The road of each day
    has many intersections
    connected to Gabe
with arrays of signposts—

—his arrival to our home and lives
    forty five years ago
—schools, teams, and games,
    parties and celebrations
—our trips to forests,
    beaches, and tide pools
—final breath—eight months ago
    minus three days.

So many trips
    some excursions now painful
    disconcerting
some awesome in their beauty,
    the reality of life well-lived
    even in three cancer-years.

Amid intersections and byways
    I seek a single thread
    a unifying continuity
and I recall
    a few weeks before cancer's end

I said, Thank you
    for being my son.
And you said, Thank you
    for being my dad.

One Refrain

Hello, Goodbye are bondings —
    nurturing and fruitful.

In our time together
    we planted fields.
        In time apart
            these grew with us.

Within Time's fertility
    the consistent refrain
        Hello, Goodbye
            keeps us inseparable.

Memorial Day

I believe today's visit to my son's memorial
    will be both sad and healing.

I believe the weather will have a slight chill,
    and I believe the nearby-restaurant food
    will be pleasantly tasty and overpriced.

I believe my heart is lost in confusion—
    thinking I may have grieved well
        since my tears now lack frequency,
    then sensing an unpredictable avalanche
        of sorrow massive and paralyzing.

I believe our imperfect words
    faltering voices, distractible minds
    will continue to provide resilience.

I believe there will be more to tell,
    just as there is more of myself
    to uncover in the telling.

I believe my son and I will continue
    our conversing . . . our communing
    in daily life with each other.

            I believe every day
            will be memorial day.

We Pick Camellias

We pick camellias
    little white ones
    gorgeous pinks
    humongous reds
my granddaughter and I.

Remembering my son, her uncle,
    we seek the best blooms.
    How joyfully
    she says his name!
Truly, he picks with us.

We seek camellias
    to celebrate tomorrow
    his birthday, without him
    almost seven months now.
We select with a pure love.

He left us a garden
    tragically incomplete
    magically growing
    a well-crafted human-scape.
This garden we will never be without.

Choosing each flower with care—
    little white ones . . .
    gorgeous pinks . . .
    humungous reds . . .
we pick camellias.

Acknowledgments

A *Crush of Wrinkles* first appeared in the *San Diego Poetry Annual* 2022-23 as a Finalist for the Steve Kowit Poetry Prize 2022.

Credits

Front Cover and **Frontispiece:** *Lake Poway Morning* photograph by KEN BUHR

Interior photos: courtesy of the Buhr family archives

Cover Design: RILEY PRATO

Book Design: ISABEL WILLIAMS

About the Poet

Poet, psychotherapist, priest, philosopher KEN BUHR has spent 48 years in private practice as a Family and Marriage Therapist in San Diego's North County Inland. He earned a PhD from the University of Southern California in 1975.

Before that, he began a career as a Catholic priest, with a Licentiate in Sacred Theology degree from the Pontifical Gregorian University in Rome in 1963. His duties included serving as a Latin stenographer for the archives of Vatican Council II for three of its four sessions.

The poet appeared later in life, at age 58. A significant voice in regional poetry, Ken is a regular contributor to the *San Diego Poetry Annual*. In 2022, he garnered Finalist honors in the Steve Kowit Poetry Prize.

Born in Los Angeles and married for 52 years, he and his wife Deanna have four grandchildren from two sons — the oldest died of cancer in 2020, and is the central driver of this collection of poems.

A past president of the Rancho Bernardo Chamber of Commerce and past chairman of the American Cancer Society board in north county San Diego, Ken is a cancer survivor himself.

Unsure of what's next in what he refers to as "this awesome multi-layered human life," Ken likes to think along the lines of Stanley Kunitz in *Layers*: "I am not done with my changes."

Made in the USA
Columbia, SC
22 August 2023

21885634R00065